LAURLYN LOVER

Wrapped

In A

Ribbon

A Selection Of
Inspirational Writings

By Flavia Weedn

Roserich Designs, Ltd.
Carpinteria, California

Library of Congress Cataloging in Publication Data

WRAPPED IN A RIBBON
Printed In Italy
ISBN 0-913289-10-8

*This book is dedicated
to those of you, like me,
who believe in life and love —
and the strength and courage
found in the human spirit.*

*Life
is
a
miracle
and
the right
to live
is
a gift.
It's
wrapped
in a ribbon
woven
with dreams . . .*

*. . . and
whether
you are
very young
or very old . . .*

*. . . life
is filled
with
wonder
and surprises.*

◆ ◆ ◆

The
winter moon
smiles
in the
heavens
and
quietly hides
tomorrow
like
a secret.

◆　◆　◆

There
will always
be
places
in our
hearts
to build
castles
in.

◆ ◆ ◆

Hope,
like love,
transcends
all time.
It is
a friend,
a healer,
a maker
of
dreams.

◆ ◆ ◆

*Gathered
leaves
wear coats
of
many
colours . . .*

*. . . and
each
one
is painted
by
Time.*

◆ ◆ ◆

*Music
bridges
the silence
when
our words
are
empty
of hand.*

◆ ◆ ◆

*While
we walk
through
the pages
of Time,
life offers
loveliness
for sale.*

◆ ◆ ◆

*"And
what is
as important
as knowledge?"
asked the mind.
"Caring and seeing
with the heart,"
answered
the soul.*

◆ ◆ ◆

*That
which
brings us
sadness
has
once
brought
us
joy.*

*May
you
cherish
forever
all that
was
yours.*

◆   ◆   ◆

Life's
gifts
are
scattered
in abundance
for all
our
hearts
to see.

◆　◆　◆

Be
a searcher.
Those
who seek
are
the finders
of
treasures.

◆　◆　◆

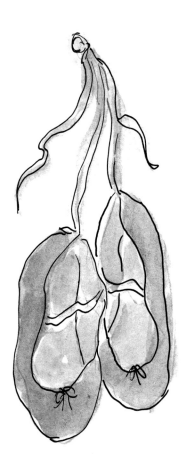

Life
is brief
and
very fragile.
Do that
which
makes
you
happy.

◆　◆　◆

*Each
of us
is
a part
of
all that
surrounds
us . . .*

*. . . and
every
joy
we feel
is
a celebration
of
life.*

◆ ◆ ◆

Only
when
you
give
do you
harvest
the abundance
of love
life
offers.

◆ ◆ ◆

Only
you
can
awaken
the
sleeping
giant
within
you.

◆ ◆ ◆

Maybe
all of life's
promises
don't
come true,
but
the mornings
still come
and hopes,
like sparrows,
still sing
in the trees.

◆ ◆ ◆

*Be
unafraid
to show
gentleness . . .*

BUBBLES

*. . . for that
is where
life's
greatest
strength
is found.*

◆   ◆   ◆

*Life's
greatest
values
are
intangible
and
never
seen
by
the eye.*

❖ ❖ ❖

*Some people
come
into our lives
and
quickly go.*

Some stay
for awhile,
leave footprints
on our hearts,
and we
are never, ever
the same.

◆　◆　◆

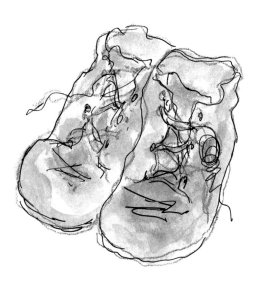

*Deep
inside
all
new
beginnings
there
breathes
a song
of
hope.*

◆ ◆ ◆

*In every
single
moment
there is
significance...*

*. . . and every
ordinary thing
is bursting
with its own
beauty.*

◆ ◆ ◆

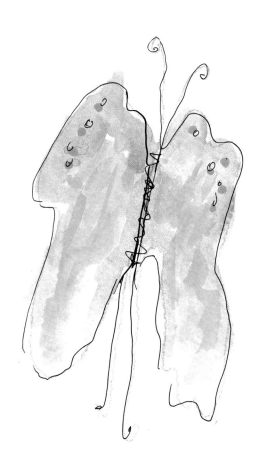

Sometimes
we must
understand . . .
. . . it is
not
necessary
to
understand.

◆　◆　◆

*Our pain
can
become
a
bridge
to a
deeper
awakening.*

◆ ◆ ◆

*Feel
sadness
so that
you
may know
happiness . . .
. . . lest
you
overlook
it.*

◆ ◆ ◆

*It is
never easy
reaching
for dreams.
Strength
and courage
can sometimes
be lonely
friends . . .*

*. . . but
those
who dream
walk
in
stardust.*

◆　◆　◆

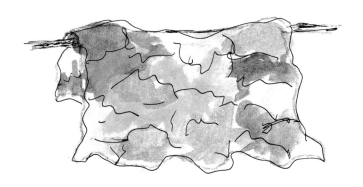

*Our lives
are
woven
by
the weavers
of Time . . .
. . . in a pattern
we cannot
see.*

◆   ◆   ◆

Be
free
to be
what
your heart
yearns
to be.

♦ ♦ ♦

*When
we
take time
to touch
the
Earth
we feel
the
closeness
of
God.*

♦ ♦ ♦

*Angels
are
all
around
us
and
every
heart
that
yearns to . . .*

*. . . can
reach
out
and
touch
a
wing.*

◆ ◆ ◆

*Much music
is found
in dreaming . . .
. . . and
the tickets
are free
for each dance.*

◆ ◆ ◆

*Heaven
smiles
softly
and hears
every
wish.*

◆ ◆ ◆

*Be
unafraid
to be.
The spirit
within
us all
is love.*

❖   ❖   ❖

*Believe
in yourself
and don't
be afraid
to take
the risk of living.*

*Each
of us
is important
and has
something
to give.*

◆ ◆ ◆

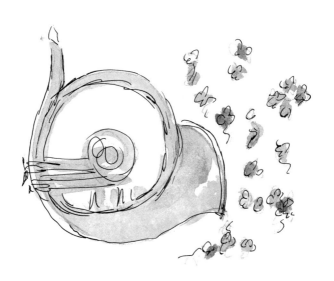

*God
gives us
music.
We are
our own
instruments.*

◆ ◆ ◆

*Thinking
is a way
of reflecting.
It becomes
a most
beautiful
habit.*

◆ ◆ ◆

*You
are made
of life.
Celebrate
the gifts
within you.*

◆   ◆   ◆

*Our time
on Earth
is made of
infinite moments,
each one
becoming another . . .*

*. . . yet each
with its own
beauty
and its own
newness.*

◆　◆　◆

*Life
is a
series
of
new beginnings.*

❖ ❖ ❖

The End

Flavia Weedn makes her home in Santa Barbara, California with her husband Jack and a big white cat named Charlie. She enjoys her family, her work, and the simple things in life.

Flavia has been painting and writing professionally for over 25 years but her work of late is truly her finest. Being a writer as well as an illustrator puts incredible demands on her time, however the endless deadlines never seem to scatter her. Painting and writing are Flavia's private passions, and she eagerly retreats daily into her octagonal studio, vintage 1940. French windows look out upon an acre of trees and a meadow overlooking the ocean. This brings her pleasure and allows her to gather her thoughts calmly while she absorbs the brilliance of this area she has chosen for her home; her beloved Santa Barbara.

When asked what her work represents she says quietly, "The incredibility of life that I feel; the beauty I see in ordinary moments and the need for people to express themselves honestly. In short, I try to bring hope to the human spirit."

Other Flavia titles include *Softly in Silver Sandals* and *The Prize, a collection of seven vignettes*. Each are available through Roserich Designs, Ltd., P O Box 1030, Carpinteria, CA 93013. Flavia is currently working on a library of collected writings.

If you wish to know more about Flavia, please write to:
The Flavia Collectors' Club, P O Box GG, Carpinteria, CA 93013